Anonymous

A true representation to the King and people of England:

How matters were carried on all along in Ireland by the late King James in

favour of the Irish papists there: from his accession to the crown, to the

tenth of April, 1689

Anonymous

A true representation to the King and people of England:
*How matters were carried on all along in Ireland by the late King James in favour of
the Irish papists there: from his accession to the crown, to the tenth of April, 1689*

ISBN/EAN: 9783337723576

Printed in Europe, USA, Canada, Australia, Japan

Cover: Foto ©ninafisch / pixelio.de

More available books at **www.hansebooks.com**

A True Reprefentation to the King and People of *England*, how Matters were carried on all a-long in *Ireland*, by the Late King *James*, in Favour of the *Irifh* *Papifts* there, *&c.*

TO fatisfie thofe that make it their bufinefs to reflect on the *Proteftants* who left *Ireland* in the late Calamities ; the following *Reafons* are briefly offered.
 Firft, It is clearly evident, That *Ireland* is a Kingdom depending on *England*, and that the Acts paffed in it are to be altered, amended, and confirmed by the King and Council of *England*, as by *Poyning*'s Act in *Ireland*, may more fully appear. That *England* receiv'd K. *J.* as their lawful King, is likewife granted; and that *Ireland* intirely fubmitted, is evident : And here I will not enter into a tedious difcourfe of all the meafures taken fince 1660, to fubvert the *Proteftant* Religion, and the Laws Eftablifhed, (*which will be fhortly at large fet forth*, by another Hand, *to the full fatisfaction of every Impartial and Unprejudiced perfon*) but briefly and truly give an account of the Proceedings in *Ireland* fince his Acceffion to the Crown. It is plain, that his whole endeavours were bent to introduce Popery, and eftablifh it in thefe Kingdoms, and that he cou'd not more re ;dily effect it, and try the Genius of his *Proteftant* Subjects of *Ireland* (who were taught to yield him Paffive Obedience, by the eafie compliance of fome of their Party then in power, to his fierce Incroachments) than by a new modelling of the Army there ; which in a very little time was fo purged, that fcarce a true *Proteftant*, or honeft Gentleman was left in it : And tho' it began by degrees whilft his Excellency the Lord *Clarendon* had the Sword, yet it was fully executed (to the almoft ruine of many a worthy Gentleman, whofe fortune depended on it) a little

after

after the Lord *Tyrconnel* had the honour of being his Deputy in that Kingdom. This being the firſt ſtep, the *Iriſh* were
made Officers, and Troops and Companies filled every
where with them, and were trained and exerciſed by an extraordinary diligence of ſome good old Officers, kept in I
ſuppoſe of purpoſe for it, who ſoon became, not only con-
temners of their *Proteſtant* Commanders, but were preferred
to their places. So that the Sword (and conſequently the Mi-
litary command of that Kingdom) was wholly in their power.   The next thing to be looked into was the Civil Magi-
ſtrate, and he who was known to be a true *Proteſtant*, was
laid aſide, and new Judges of the right ſtamp were firſt
Coyned, who had command in their reſpective Circuits to
inform the Government of all *Proteſtant Juſtices* (or *Crom-
well*'s favorers as they called them) who were likewiſe pre-
ſently eaſed of their Commiſſions, and all other Imploy-
ments. Then the Officers of the Revenue were alſo purged ;
and ſeveral of the *Iriſh* who had got in among them (in infe-
riour Stations) yet in regard they were not ſo well qualified
as the *Proteſtants*, by a knowledge in thoſe affairs, ſome were
removed, and the moſt uſeful of the *Proteſtants* reſtored for a
while ; yet as the *Iriſh* grew skilful, the *Proteſtants* ſtill were
outed again : Matters being thus acted and the *Proteſtant No-
bility*, and many of the Gentry knowing of no better Expedient than to come into *England* (ſince they could not ſtruggle
againſt the King's will, which was a Law in *Ireland*) therefore they removed hither to make a Remonſtrance of the
Grievances of that Kingdom to the late King : and tho' they
flock'd over out of all parts, yet they prevailed ſo little to
gain any redreſs, that they ſaw plainly they could not return
into *Ireland* without apparent hazard of their Lives.

And now was it judged by the Ld. Deputy the fitteſt time
for him to put his long contrived deſigns *of Subverting the
Proteſtant Religion, and introducing* Popery, *into full Execution* ;
upon which in *November* laſt, there was a motion made in
Council for diſarming all the reſt of the *Proteſtants* of that
King-

Kingdom, which being known, and moft concluding that as foon as their Arms were taken (there being then a hot Difcourfe of a general Maffacre intended) 'twas only to leave them more naked and expofed, fo as that might have its full effect more eafily, and with lefs oppofition upon them, which alarm'd the *Proteftants* fo, that many thoufands came flocking over to avoid that fatal ftroke.   Now were the few *Proteftants* who lived difperft left to fhift for themfelves. In the mean time the Lord *Tyrconnel* (who ftill had the Sword undemanded and undifpofed of to any other) iffues new Commiffions, not only to the *Ro. Ca.* who had fome Eftates ; but to all, who were willing to ftand up for the Caufe, that were men of broken Fortunes and worfe Fame, but could influence the Rabble and raife Companies, only with this Salvo, that they fhould maintain them for 3 months on their own coft and charge, and then they fhould have their Commiffions given them : by which it was adjudged, that in regard there was but little Money in the Treafury, they fhould be fitted for fervice againft the time K. *J.* fhould come, or fend them Money ; or, that if the Deputy found an Army ready to Land out of *England,* what Money was there would be little enough to bear his Charges, and furnifh him with Neceffaries on his flight. But thefe Commiffions (or rather Incouragements) being very many, for every one who could get about 60 *Kearnes,* or Country Fellows to joyn with them, and own him as their Captain, immediately ftrutted and looked very big, and was honoured, by the name of Captain ; fo that it was nothing ftrange to have 20 or 30 Companies in a County, and thefe the noted Idlers and Cow-ftealers. So that prefently the Captains (many of which had not 3 Cows of their own) had feveral fcores of Cattle driven into Nooks and By-Paths ; and all that were branded, were fure to go to Pot, in regard the *Horne* (as they called it) fpoke *Englifh* ; the reft were fent into other remote *Counties* to the Officers there, and thofe again fent their ftolen Cattle in exchange

for

for the other (which was done to elude a Proclamation from the Lord Deputy on the many and daily Complaints and Petitions he receiv'd on account of the ftolen Cattle) requiring all Officers and Soldiers as well as others to be aiding and affifting to recover the ftolen Cattle, and to punifh the Offenders; which pafs'd for currant. For it was well if a *Proteftant* could go fafe to the Captain of the next Garrifon, who fometimes would be fo civil (efpecially if a Sum of money were given his men to affift in the fearch)as to fend 8 or 10 miles, but be fure the Cattle muft be far enough from the place fearched; and fometime when 30 or 40 good fat Bullocks came to be made a Prey, that about a 3d or 4th part muft be laid afide for the Pot; the reft for a Bribe of 5 or 6 *l.* would be got by fome of the Soldiers, who would fwear luftily they were forced to promife fo much to their Spy: Yet no fooner (on the delivery of the greater part of the Cattle, and the money receiv'd) but be fure in a night or two the Cattle were again ftolen. Thus the merry Drovers (as they called themfelves) valued not to joyn about 60, or 80, or 100 in one Party, and force away what Cattle they had a mind to: fo that fometimes 100 Sheep would fcarce feed the Drivers with their Families and Friends; and a purchace of about 100, was only fit to be divided among them and their Crew into Lots and Parts, (but they called them *Steages*.) And now thefe new rais'd Forces were moft of them half armed out of the Stores, the reft were pretty well fitted for Pikes made in the Country, and the Priefts and Fryars commanded (on obedience to the Holy See) that no perfon whatfoever fhould appear at Mafs without his long *Skeane* and *Halfpike*, which accordingly was performed, and one perfon who had not one foot of Land but what he Farmed from an *Englifh* Gentleman, had 12 dozen of each made for himfelf and Tenants, an account whereof was fent the Government, but no notice taken.

And now was it judged fit that *thofe new rais'd forces* fhould
be-

betake themselves to Garrisons, which was suddainly done
---- And not only were the Kings Garrisons, Forts, and Ca-
ftles, well ftored with them, but many Gentlemens houfes
that were ftrengthy, (or whofe owners were judged dif-
affected to them) were likewife filled with their Nu nbers,
and the Proprietors, or Poffeffors turned out, and the provi-
fion feized, (and it was an extraordinary favour to get off
any Goods that were of any value) on pretence that it was
for the Kings ufe, and that he would make fatisfaction as
he thought fit, and that it was done by his Command.

Now was it plain, that this Army was not defigned to
fight with Butterflies, and that the Lives of all the *Prote-*
ftants that ftayed, were in apparent danger : On which an
humble requeft was made to one or two perfons of greateft
Quality and Station, to ftand up for the *Proteftant Religion*.
---- But either through too much Loyalty, or judging the
fcattered and difperfed *Proteftants*, too weak to withftand
their fhock, (much lefs to difarm the Party defigned) was
therefore declined and judged unfit to attempt as they pro-
pofed, feizing the Sword, Lord Deputy, and *Dublin*.

Matters being thus tranfacted, it was judged by the
Proteftant Gentry of the *Weft* of *Ireland*, that in regard *Sligoe*,
(which is a Sea-port Town, and the chief in the County)
one of the beft Pofts and ftrongeft, being alfo well fituated
to pafs from the *North* to *Connaght* ; (the *Irifh* Company a
little before being drawn out of it to a General Rendez-
vouz) and many of their new raifed Forces poffeffing them
felves daily of the moft confiderable ftrengths in the County, as *Belahy, Moygara*, which belongs to the L. *Kingfton* and
his Tenants, *Oufted*, and *Ballymoate* ; therefore, left they
fhould likewife poffefs themfelves of *Sligo* as they intended,
it was refolved by the *Proteftants* there to enter it, and poffefs themfelves of it for their defence and fafety : and fo they
did unanimoufly iffue their Declaration on the 4th day of
Jan ar. laft that they affociated themfelves in the neceffary
defence of their Lives and the *Proteftant Religion as by Law*
efta-

established, which to their utmost powers they would maintain, and would not prejudice even *Roman Catholicks* whilst
they demeaned themselves according to the Laws ---The
Protestants then chose the Right Honorable *Robert* L. Baron
of *Kingstone,* and the Honor. *Chidley Coote,* Esq; their Commanders in chief, to whom they promised intire obedience.
---And accordingly all were formed into Troops and Companies, and all furnished themselves with the Men under
their respective Commands, with Horses, Arms, Ammunition, Provisions, &c. imploying all the Smiths in fixing
Arms, making Pikes, Stars, and other Inventions against
Horse, and to defend Forts, buying all the Scythes, and fixing them on Poles, building up the old and decayed Forts,
making Draw bridges, ordering frontier Garrisons, keeping
strong Watch and Ward on all Quarters, at *Grange* near
Mid-way to *Balishannon,* to hold their Correspondence with
Derry, at *New-town, Dromahere,* and *Mannerhamelton,* to have
intelligence with *Enniskilling,* at Dr. *Leslies,* at *Coolooni,* and
Marcray, to prevent an infal from the *Boyle,* or *Ballymoate*; at
Ardinglafs, Lackan, and *Cottlestovn,* to awe the new rais'd
Army in the County of *Mayo,* part of which had seized
the Bishop of *Killalla's* House: And when one Mr. *Trem-
ble* (a Servant of Sir *Arthur Gore's*) ask'd one Captain
Walter Bourke why he would seize the Bishop's House,
and make it a Garrison, the Gate was shut upon him,
and he set upon and barbarously murthered. Likewise
an Account of the Protestants, who were at *Foxford,*
and many other places, who were drawing to *Sligo* on
the Orders that issued for disarming all Protestants of the
Kingdom; as also to take all their Service-Horses, which
was obeyed with that Secrecy, Diligence, and Care, that
not so much as a Plow-Horse was left; so that many a Family, for want of a Horse to carry their Luggage, was
forced to stay and submit to their merciless Cruelty; but
this Garrison relieved and conveyed many a distressed
and robbed Protestant to *Sligo,* who soon was recruited
                     and

and put into Troop or Company at the Officers coſt. During this time there was a ſecret Intreague with Secretary *Ellis* and Mr. *Temple* : As alſo a ſham Letter from the Lord *Tyrconel* into *England* about delivering the Sword ; and had there one been ſent to demand the Sword with about a Thouſand Soldiers, 'tis not doubted but it would be delivered; though at the ſame time the Lord *Montjoy* (leaſt he ſhould ſtand up for the Proteſtants) is Complemented with an Embaſſy into *France.*

And now the *Iriſh* getting all this time to ſtrengthen themſelves, and the Arms and Horſes taken from the Proteſtants, they began to encreaſe to an Army of 90000. ſtrong : And all this while there was neither Commiſſion, Arms, Ammunition, or Money ſent to the Proteſtants at *Sligo,* notwithſtanding that as they were Informed, it was earneſtly ſollicited by a Perſon of Quality in *England,* who knew the goodneſs and ſtrength of that Poſt they were in, and that they daily expected ſome Succours, ſo that the Proteſtants there began to be in very great want of Ammunition ; and notwithſtanding all their endeavours, wanted many Arms, tho' all the fowling Pieces were cut into Carbines, and Smiths continually at work. And the Sword (to which the Supreme Acknowledgment is paid) was ſtill undemanded in the Lord *Tyrconnel's* hand, and ſure without Command he would not lay it down ; yet the Proteſtants at *Sligo* continued in their own and Proteſtant Religions defence, according to their Declaration of the Fourth of *January,* without any violation of it, and kept conſtant Watch and Ward with the uſual Exerciſe againſt occaſion offered, only on account of ſeveral Proteſtants who were ſtopt at *Boile,* and their Goods ſeiz'd by Colonel *Mac Donel,* who poſſeſt himſelf of my Lord *Kingſton's* Houſe there, and likewiſe on all the Corn and Hay of his Tenants near it. The

B   ſaid

said Lord *Kingston* writ to the Colonel, defiring him
to let the Proteftants with their Goods come down, for
he did not hinder any Papift to remove to him ; which
not being done , my Lord refolved to deliver thofe
from their Reftraints, and accordingly with a confiderable Party of Horfe and Foot marched to *Boile*; but
the Colonel hearing of my Lord's coming, drew in all
his Men and Horfes into my Lord's Houfe and Court,
and Capitulated, and let his Prifoners go ; and enga-
ged on Honour not to hinder any from joyning at
Sligo; but no fooner was my Lord and his Party gone,
than the next day thofe that heard of that Engage-
ment, and were defirous to go thither, were all feized
and kept clofe Prifoners till the Affizes—— About this
time, which was the 12*th* of *March*, the unlucky Declaration (pardon the Expreffion) of the Second of
February laft, as being fent before any Army was Landed to back it, and was there receiv'd, which gave time
to all Papifts to lay down their Arms and repair to their
refpective Dwellings by the 10*th* of *April* laft, &c.
which did fo tye up all the Proteftants from offering
Violence, even to thofe who fome time before ftole
their Cattel, that the leaft Violence was not offered
them, in an abfolute and intire Obedience to that Declaration ; by which means they were encouraged to
have pardon for their Villanies and Robberies, and told
by the Priefts, Fryars and Officers, that no Army would
be fent to fupprefs them: and therefore till the time li-
mited, they fhould let none know their Refolutions,
whether to lay down, or ftand to their Arms.—— Alfo
the *French* Marquefs *Dupont*-landing in *Kinfale*, and
going to *Dublin* about this time, was fplendidly enter-
tain'd there by the Lord Deputy, who affured him it
would not be long till an Army Landed in *Ireland* out
of *France*, as alfo of King *James's* going thither very
                                                    fpeedily,

speedily, and a full account of what since hapned, which would not at all be credited by any Proteſtants, but that an Army would land out of *England* before any could come from *France*; but it was hoped the Marqueſs would not return back to *France* nor ſcape our Men at Sea —— Intelligence being now receiv'd, and Account of the Army, and how Affairs ſtood, being ſent back by Monſieur, it was judged expedient to march an Army with all ſpeed to the *North*, and ſuppreſs the Proteſtants there. Accordingly an Army came to *Liſnegarvy* which (after a little Diſpute, a great number of their Men falling on a ſmall Party of ours) made them quit their Ground. —— The noiſe of this Victory ſoon took wing, and gave them encouragement to Beſiege *Colerain*; and not being able to do any Execution on that ſide, drew off their Men to march them back to get over the Bridge above it, and ſo fall on that Town from the other ſide of the River, on which *Colerain* wanting truſty and good Officers in it to Command, the Rabble with the Inhabitants deſerted and left the Town, (excepting only thoſe that reſolved to ſubmit to the Enemy) by which means, and the great diſorder they were in to get to *Derry*, many a good Horſe and Arms, as well as the Riches of that Town, fell into the Enemies hands. —— Notice of theſe Diſaſters being immediately ſent from *Derry* by Colonel *Lundee* to the Gentlemen, who kept Garriſons in their Houſes in the Counties of *Monaghan*, *Cavan*, &c. who were earneſtly deſired to draw down immediately with their Men, and joyn *Derry* Men; and underſtanding the Condition *Derry* was in, marcht forthwith: And left the Enemy ſhould poſſeſs themſelves of their ſtrong Houſes, Goods, and Proviſions, ſet fire to all, and marcht away by the light of it; conſuming their own Goods and Houſes, to joyn with *Derry* Men, and op-

poſe

pose the Enemies marching thither to besiege it. And
though it might be judged, the Loyalty and Zeal of
these Gentlemen need not be question'd; yet hitherto
there is but small Provisions made for them. And if it
be asked what made them come over, 'tis easily answe-
red, the Divisions in *Derry* amongst several there, (who
hitherto have scaped being called to account for it,
may be fear'd, were private Instruments) and who took
on them the Command, and ordered Matters as they
themselves pleased, taking no advice but that of their
own Pleasures, gave such plain occasion of distrust,
that it was judged better by those and other honest
Gentlemen there, to come over and give an Account
how matters were, than to stay in disorder and Confusion, when especially they were not able to stem the
Current that so violently run against them, and whose
business it was to joyn and assist with the Governour,
rather than to give him publick opposition, when private Advice proved vain; so that as well to avoid mu-
tinying with him, as to bring a Calumny on themselves,
to be so much as suspected for betraying that Interest
and Religion they were not able to defend or pre-
serve, the Rabble being in Confusion, who sometime
would have one, another day another Officer; and sometime would joyn themselves, and do as they pleased.
The one part of Protestants deserting the other, and
these not able to withstand the Enemy without mutual
assistance; and if they could, not daring to trust their
Governour, who was there (as well as he had been at
Colerain) when they were about seizing him, and shut
the Gates on him that he should not get away, till by
his Oaths of Fidelity to them, (which he freely gave)
and a little Policy, he got off; and being under vehe-
ment Suspicions of a private Correspondence with
King *James,* who about this time was in *Dublin,* had
crea-

created such great Jealousies, Feuds and Heart-burnings in the Soldiers, he refusing to give the Command to him chosen by the People: which was of no small Advantage to the Enemy, and daily weakned the Town, by the Desertion of those who durst neither trust him, nor themselves under his Command.

During these disorders, Letters came to *Sligo* by Expresses one after another from the Colonel, desiring my Lord *Kingston* to send a Party to join them at *Derry*. But answer being immediately return'd him, that there were not men enow at *Sligo* to keep that Post (so far from all relief and) in the Face of the Enemy, and of the want there was of Arms and Ammunition (which were then at *Derry* to be had for Money.) Every Officer for himself and Men, sent for so many as they wanted, according to their Proportions, and made a Purse, and thought it convenient to send Captain *Coote* forthwith to acquaint them with the state of the Garrison and know theirs; — and bring Arms and Ammunition, which were very much wanting; — whilst another Letter came posting, to desire a speedy joining them at *Derry*. But a Council being call'd, it was resolved to stay till Captain *Coote* returned and brought the certainty how Matters were, and not to quit that advantageous Post lightly, which cost so much Money and Work to strengthen it, and had so many Men, Women and Children, that had from almost all parts of *Connaght* flockt to it, and could not get room, nor be provided for at *Derry*; and above all, was so considerable to awe all *Connaght* Forces, that in case of Hardships, Succours could come by Sea, which were now daily expected by every blast of an Easterly Wind, which was heartily wish'd and greedily long'd for. But streight a third Express was suddenly hastened, shewing the great Danger the *North* was in; and if that were lost, (as it was feared, without *Sligo*-Forces joining them, it would)

that

that *Sligo* could not hold out long after, and earneftly defired to defert it ; and that he had provided Quarters and Forrage ready for them there, and come immediately to their relief. On which Exprefs another Council was held, and knowing the great want there was of Ammunition (not much above one Barrel of Powder being in the Garrifon at *Sligo*,)and the Danger that threatnes them at *Derry*, it was refolv'd to join them forthwith, and quit *Sligo*, and to put all to the fhort Ifue of one Field-Fight. Accordingly all now refolved to march with Bag and Baggage. The next day was fpent in providing Horfes and Neceffaries, in getting Boats, breaking the big Guns, and fending of the fmall to *Derry* by Water ; burning and deftroying all the Corn, Hay, and Haggards about the Country ; calling in all the Frontier Garrifons; —— and every one ufing his utmoft endeavours (fome by Water to the Ifland of *Enifhmorrey*, that was judged capable of defence till the Goods and Men could get off by Water to *Derry*,) the reft with what Horfes they could get : fo that the day following all marched ; and a Veffel lying then at *Sligo*, as many as could get off, with fome Goods, the Wind being fair, failed away. But after two daies March (in the faddeft Weather that could blow,) coming to *Belafhannon*, 20 miles from *Sligo*, a fourth Letter comes to my Lord, to ftay him there till Quarters were provided for him, and Forrage got for Horfes; which was no fmall furprize, after drawing him from his Poft, on Affurance of providing thofe neceffaries, and of the diftrefs that threatned *Derry*.

A Boat alfo with Paffengers and Goods from *Sligo* was caft away near *Donigale*, and another fent with the Fieldpieces,by reafon of the Storm put into an *Ifland*, and the next day feiz'd and taken back, as were all the Goods, Provifions, Men, and Women that went into the Ifland, which was no fmall Booty. —— But now was my Lord
Kingfton

Kingston forced, for want of Forrage, to difperfe his Men, fome to *Beleeke*, fome to *Donigale*, fome to *Killabegs* (to keep *Boylagh* men in Awe, who were extreamly increafed, and began to rob publickly on *Barnefmore*,) fome at *Belafhannon*, and fome about the County; and fo continued for feventeen days in a very ill condition for want of Forrage, many of the Horfes being turned to Grafs for want of it, and the Weather continuing extreamly bad; which fo abufed them, that many were made unferviceable.—— At length a Letter comes from the Colonel to my Lord to *Belafhannon* about ten at night, to fecure the Pafs at *Ballymofey* (30 Miles thence) by ten next day, which was altogether impoffible to be done;——neither could it be (under half that time) that the men could have notice of it, fent them, as they lay fcattered in their feveral Quarters, which formerly I mentioned; and many were likewife to provide Horfes, their own being dead, or fo weak and out of Condition for want of Forrage, that they were of little ufe for ervice : However two Companies that were at and near *Donnigale*, march'd in the Morning betime to join the *Northern* Men, and to fecure that Pafs, which was 20. Miles from them, and many hundreds of Men, Women and Children march'd with them, with Bag and Baggage in hopes to get to *Derry* before the Enemy intercepted them; but this day being difmally wet, and extream windy, and marching over that horrible Mountain of *Barnefmore*, which is 15 miles long, tho' they marched at an extraordinary rate, yet it was feven at night before they could reach it; and my Lord (expecting to meet Colonel *Lundy* there) rid with a dozen Horfe, to difcourfe him, and to know why he was drawn from his Poft on pretence of fo great danger? why he kept there in that bad condition fo long after he had receiv'd his Letter, that Quarters and Forrage was provided for him

and

why he had not notice fooner fent him
the Enemies approaching fo near? and how was it
poffible for him to march his Men, who lay fcattered
at fuch a diftance, under at leaft three daies notice?
but coming thither, there was foon an account given by
thofe, who that day were broke and fled from *Cladyford*
Fight, that the Colonel, with the Horfe whom he commanded to go with him to fecure a Pafs on the River
above *Cladyford*, was gone to *Derry*; and it was not
much queftioned but the Enemy, who foon fell into
Rapho, killing Men in the very Streets there, would
be as foon at the Gate, and enter, as the Colonel.-—
And it is not much to be doubted, that had the *Irish*
Army Liberty of getting over that *Ford*, which they
could not poffibly do, without great danger of their
Lives, the Waters being fo very high with that days rain,
and the Bridge being broken down, that if they could
have marched over and purfued their Victory, they
would have got in without great (if any) oppofition;
for Colonel *Cunningham*, with the Succours fent by him
for the relief and defence of the Town, had fet fail, and
reurned: and it was not doubted but *Derry* as well as
Colerain, would be left to them by the Colonel, in regard that neither Men nor Arms were landed.——And
now this Party thus difappointed at *Ballemofey*, and the
Enemy in *Rapho* between them and *Derry*, after this
days fad March, were now forced to return that night,
over that wild Mountain; and Horfes being weak and
weary with the long March and bad weather, could
not get back that night, but were left with Loads
and all: So that by much difficulty, and by the great
care the two Companies of Foot (who brought up
the Rear) took to bring off the Women and Children, who were fadly toiled and tired, many of them
would have been left and loft, as almoft all their Goods
and

and Baggage were. —And next Morning marched to *Donnigale,* with much difficulty and distress, by reason of the badness of the Weather, as well as that of the way, and the Darknefs, Windinefs, and Rain, contributing not a little to the Hazards and Loffes they fuftained.—And now confulting what was to be done in thefe Diforders, or rather treacherous Practices, it was concluded that my Lord *Kingfton* (with the Officers of his appointment that were there with him) fhould come off in three or four Veffels that lay at *Killabeggs,* and haften over and give an account how matters were, and get Commiffions and return with all fpeed to their Friends, Relations and Tenants; whom they mounted and armed and fent ftraight to joyn *Enifkillen* Men; which was no fmall trouble to them, that after about four months coft, fufferings, and acquaintance, they muft now part, having neither Arms, Ammunition, nor Supplies fent them : but it was now plain, that the Colonel (who knew very well that King *James* was near his Army) which gave clear occafions of diftruft, and that the private under-hand intelligence he held would be to the ruin of the Proteftants; and the day after the Lord *Kingfton,* the wind being fair, fet fail. But to relate the miferies and hardfhips they endured at fea; lying a Ship-board like packt Herrings in their Boots and wet Cloaths for fix or feven days, and twice like to be caft away on the *Scotch* Shoar; and thence getting to *Glafgow* in fmall Boats, fome again riding poft to *London* with my Lord, others going to *Edinburgh,* and then by Sea, fome afoot to *Leverpool* above 200 miles, others again venturing thither by Sea, who ever fince have been waiting, petitioning, and expecting to return with Commiffions for themfelves as well as for fome of their Friends, who have given the World fatisfaction of their Courage and Zeal for the Proteftant Religion, and whofe Names ought to be honoured with a perpetual

C   Remem-

Remembrance of their Actions. · And if the Archbishop of *Tuam* or Bishop of *Killalla*, who very well knows my Lord, with the Gentlemen that came over with him, and what they did and suffered whilst they were at *Sligo*, be enquired of the truth of this matter, that certainly persons who are provided for, and who never shewed that Zeal would not be preferred, and these (not only neglected, by which means they suffer many hardships, but) even discountenanced, by being called Deserters of their Country ; and whether this usage be not a Trial of their Zeal, I leave to any one to judge : also on due enquiry, or after what is said, if they for coming over, or the Person who drew them from their Post, who by their Majesties Commission, was Governour of *Derry*, and who hazarded their Lives and Fortunes to join with him, without Commissions to oppose the Enemy, to be so served, or he be most to blame?— Or whether they who know the Mountains, Creeks and Passes, as well as the notorious bloody Rebels and Cow-stealers, who have most of their nearest Relations, either hazarding their Lives against them, or under their Power, at least in restraint, with cruel usage and hardships enough, if they have yet escaped with their Lives: whether also that these Gentlemen, who have left their Goods, and come over, some with a very little Money, Plate, or other Moveables of value, which is now all spent ; and some who have a great Charge of eight or ten in Family, who in probability might have starved many of them, had not that charitable Course been taken for their support ; that is, who cannot raise Money here for want of City-security ; neither their own (tho they have good Estates in *Ireland*) nor the Gentlemen thence to be taken bound for them; whether, I say, these be able to return for want of Horses, Arms, or Necessaries to carry them over, having spent all, and to carry a Musket, and leave their Families in want, and wholly unsettled and wanting Bread, would
                                                            not

not only be bad encouragement for them, but that Pay would neither maintain them, nor fcarce any one of their Familie; and whether a due confideration and regard be not to be had of thofe fo quallified for Employments, and Perfons of known Courage and Zeal for the Proteftant Religion, of whom there are many unprovided for of a-ny Employment; which would be a great eafe to *England* in the feveral Sums paid for the Relief of thofe Prote-ftants, who are now here in no capacity nor ability for providing for themfelves, tho they are fufficiently zea-lous for their Majefties Service.

And whether a farther delay may not be prejudicial as Matters ftand, confidering that for want of a fpeedy relieving of *Ireland*, and not fending over but about 100. Officers, and one to Command in Chief, with Arms, Ammunition, Commiffions, and Money in *Ja-nuary*, *February*, *March*, or *April* laft, that Kingdom had not been wholly in the Proteftants hands, notwith-ftanding all the French Army fince Landed, as well as that raifed by *Tyrconnel*, and if it had not prevented the ruin, Deftruction, Defolation, and Cruelties, which the Proteftants there have fince fuffered?

And now 'tis hoped it may not be amifs to infpect and enquire who the Retarders are; and to do it fo effectu-ally, that they at length be fruftrated of carrying on any farther Defigns, to the Apparent ruin of the Pro-teftants, and to bring them to Condign Punifhments for the Blood and Miferies many Thoufands have fuffe-red by the *Irifh* and *French* Cruelties, who were the Inftruments who occafion'd it. And whether they did not endeavour by fuch Practices to Eftablifh Popery, as well as Confufion.

May they therefore be found out and made Exam-ples for their Perfidy. May their Sacred Majefties ever be happy and defend the Proteftant Reli-gion from Popery and Superftition; and have the
Hearts

Hearts of all their Subjects intirely united to them, whilft all *Achitophels* juftly fuffer. May *England* with all their Majefties Kingdoms and Dominions flourifh under Peace and Safety, whilft we Blefs God for his great Deliverances he wrought for us, in Placing their Majefties on the Royal Throne. May the Poor Proteftants of *Ireland* Blefs the Almighty, who they hope hath raifed a Deliverer for them, that they may return in Peace to enjoy their Poffeffions ; that they may make the right and Sanctified ufe of their Afflictions, fo that they and their Children may never forget the great Deliverances wrought for them : Whilft the *Irifh* and *French* be turned out of that Land, and receive their juft demerits, and that Religion and true Piety, may ever flourifh and be eftablifh'd among us for all Generations. And may *Duke Schomberg* have this alfo added to his former Renowned Acts, to prove the Deliverer, firft of the *Irifh* Proteftants, and then of the *French* in *France*.

F I N I S.

Books lately Printed for *Ric. Chifwell.*

THe Anfwer of a Proteftant Gentleman in *Ireland*, to a late Letter from *N. N.* upon a Difcourfe betwixt them concerning the prefent Pofture of that Countrey, and the Part fit for thofe concerned there to Act in it.

An Aplogy for the Proteftants in *Ireland*, in a Brief Narrative of the late Revolutions in that Kingdom, and an Account of the Prefent State thereof.

The Intereft of *England* in the Prefervation of *Ireland*, Humbly prefented to the Parliament of *England* by *G. P.* Efq;

There is in the Prefs, and will be fhortly Publifhed

A Full and Impartial Account of all the Secret Confults, Negotiations, Stratagems, and Intrigues of the *Remifh Party* in Ireland, from 1660 to this prefent year 1689. for the Settlement of Popery in that Kingdom.